Would You Rather Book For Kids
401 Questions For Kids, Teens, and Their Parents

1. *Would you rather*...choose to have a superpower of flying whenever you are happy, or choose to be invisible whenever you wish?

2. *Would you rather*...turn the entire year into summer and spend as much time on the beach and sunbathing, or turn the year into a long and snowy winter and get 365 days for skiing, ice skating and snowball fights?

3. *Would you rather*...know what each new day would exactly bring or live without knowing and always be surprised?

4. *Would you rather*...read other people's minds, or have everyone know what you like and don't like without ever having to ask?

5. *Would you rather*...have a robot that can help you with everything, or be a robot and have no impossible tasks?

6. *Would you rather*...watch TV whenever you wanted or get to skip classes that you don't like?

7. *Would you rather*...be the best at one thing, or know a little bit of everything about anything?

8. *Would you rather*...choose to speak and understand every language in the world or make up your own language that everyone would want to learn?

9. *Would you rather*...become the strongest person on earth or choose to be the smartest human that ever lived?

10. *Would you rather*...have the power to freeze the time whenever you feel like it, or have a time machine and go back in time?

11. *Would you rather*...have to do tests every day in school, or go to school even on weekends?

12. *Would you rather*...never to go to a class that you don't like, or make Fridays a part of the weekend?

13. *Would you rather*...stay up late whenever you like, or have your favorite dinner every day?

14. *Would you rather*...be a straight-A student, or be the best athlete in your school?

15. *Would you rather*...do the dishes every day, or have to clean the toilet every week?

16. *Would you rather*...get to play your favorite game every day for as long as you like, or get to live in a game once a week?

17. *Would you rather*...know what will happen in the future, or get to choose what won't happen?

18. *Would you rather*...would you rather have to wear boots, or sandals for the rest of your life?

19. *Would you rather*...have a pet elephant, or a pet giraffe?

20. *Would you rather*...be able to have an X-ray vision and see through walls, or be able to go through the walls?

21. *Would you rather...*kiss a toad, or hold a snake around your neck?

22. *Would you rather...*have to sing instead of talking or speak in rhymes your entire life?

23. *Would you rather...*eat pizza every day forever, or have French fries instead of meals you don't like?

24. *Would you rather...*have bad grades and be the most popular kid in your school, or be the smartest kid in school with top grades?

25. *Would you rather...*have cherry-flavored tears or sneeze strawberry milkshake?

26. *Would you rather...*travel the whole world in only several weeks, or be able to visit your favorite cities and countries whenever you wish?

27. *Would you rather*...have a single best friend, or have many friends that like you but are not that close to you?

28. *Would you rather*...choose to be a wizard or a witch, or a werewolf or a vampire?

29. *Would you rather*...have flying cockroaches, or flying snakes around?

30. *Would you rather*...be the funniest kid in your school, or the prettiest?

31. *Would you rather*...have to wear clown's pants every day or a clown wig once a week?

32. *Would you rather*...know how every book ends without having to read it, or be able to read any book in only few hours?

33. *Would you rather*...have wings, or be able to breathe underwater?

34. *Would you rather*...understand what animals think and say, or have animals understand what you are saying?

35. *Would you rather*...have the nights last longer during the entire year, or have longer daytime?

36. *Would you rather*...ride a unicorn, or fly a dragon?

37. *Would you rather*...be able to manipulate fire, or be able to control water?

38. *Would you rather*...have all your food taste salty no matter what you eat, or have it taste sweet?

39. *Would you rather*...pick to eat potatoes in all forms for every meal,

or have a meal that you don't like for every dinner?

40. *Would you rather*...eat broccoli every day for lunch or eat an entire onion every year?

41. *Would you rather*...have to move by only running everywhere you go, or be forced to skip your way around like a rabbit?

42. *Would you rather*...be lost in a forest with a map on your side, or be stranded in the middle of the ocean in a boat?

43. *Would you rather*...be the fastest person in the world, but only when you are scared, or be the strongest only when you are angry?

44. *Would you rather*...never have to brush your teeth again, or never have to take a shower again?

45. *Would you rather*...be a part of a losing team where you are the best player, or be the worst player in the winning team?

46. *Would you rather*...eat a burger that tastes like vanilla ice cream, or eat ice cream that tastes like burgers?

47. *Would you rather*...live in the time of the dinosaurs, or live in the Middle Ages?

48. *Would you rather*...live in the world where electricity was never discovered and used, or live in the world where flushing toilets and toothpaste were never invented?

49. *Would you rather*...have no hair at all and be entirely bald, or have fur-like hair all over your body?

50. *Would you rather*...never to watch TV again, or never to go out and play with your friends?

51. *Would you rather*...entirely lose your sense of smell, or only be able to recognize bad smell?

52. *Would you rather*...live in North Pole, or somewhere in a tropical rainforest?

53. *Would you rather*...have everyone know when you are nervous, or have everyone able to notice when you are sad?

54. *Would you rather*...meet Bigfoot or the Loch Ness monster?

55. *Would you rather*...walk through a forest alone at night, or be stranded in the middle of the desert during daytime?

56. *Would you rather*...have a really pointy nose or extremely long toes?

57. *Would you rather*...never have to study again and get all straight A's, or never have to get up early in the morning and still be on time for school?

58. *Would you rather*...have spinach soup for breakfast every day, or have cold showers forever instead?

59. *Would you rather*...live in an underground city, or live on the top of the tallest peak of a mountain?

60. *Would you rather*...turn everything you touch into gold, or have a path of roses growing wherever you walk?

61. *Would you rather*...have your favorite actor or actress come at your birthday party every year, or

be invited to their birthday party
only once?

62. *Would you rather*...have spaghetti
    instead of hair, or carrots instead of
    fingers?

63. *Would you rather*...have elf ears,
    or a monkey tail?

64. *Would you rather*...live in your
    favorite fantasy book, or live in your
    all-time favorite science fiction
    movies?

65. *Would you rather*...be a superhero
    with a duty to save and help
    everyone, or be friends with a
    superhero who is always there to
    help you when in need?

66. *Would you rather*...go jump with a
    parachute from a tall cliff, or go
    diving in the ocean?

67. *Would you rather*...have a bathroom full of spiders, or an entire house full of biting mosquitos?

68. *Would you rather*...read all the books in the world in a week, or write a best-selling book in ten years?

69. *Would you rather*...have a self-cleaning room, or a robot that does all your homework for you?

70. *Would you rather*...have a magical creature for a friend, or be a magical creature yourself?

71. *Would you rather*...be awful at singing but a great dancer, or awful at dancing but great at singing?

72. *Would you rather*...try to train a snake, or tame a tiger?

73. *Would you rather*...sleep with lights off in a dark room, or with lights on but with a huge spider in the room?

74. *Would you rather*...not wash your hands for a year, or not change your socks for an entire year?

75. *Would you rather*...talk in riddles for a month, or not speak at all for a week?

76. *Would you rather*...throw away your favorite toy from when you were a baby, or be unable to find your current favorite toy every once in a week for a year?

77. *Would you rather*...have a year-long supply of snacks, or a year-long supply of sweets?

78. *Would you rather*...eat everything else except for your favorite food for good, or only be allowed to eat your

favorite food but nothing else forever?

79. *Would you rather*...help with cooking dinner, or wash the dishes after dinner?

80. *Would you rather*...jump into a pool of mud, or into a pool of honey and feathers?

81. *Would you rather*...stay up late but get up really early, or go to bed on time and wake up whenever you like?

82. *Would you rather*...participate in making a movie, or making a song?

83. *Would you rather*...live in aqua park for a month, or in an amusement park?

84. *Would you rather*...travel to Mars and never get back to Earth, or visit

the Moon every month and get back home?

85. *Would you rather*...explore the deepest parts of the ocean, or head to space travels?

86. *Would you rather*...be a genius scientist, or a famous artist?

87. *Would you rather*...bathe in apple juice, or bathe in milk?

88. *Would you rather*...brush your teeth with sand, or wash your hair with ketchup?

89. *Would you rather*...pretend to be from another planet, or pretend not to understand your language?

90. *Would you rather*...spend an hour in a moving elevator, or an hour in a moving cable car?

91. *Would you rather*...be able to hear everything from a long distance, or have your voice loud enough to be heard for miles when you wish so?

92. *Would you rather*...spend a day watching TV but not be allowed to play outside for a week, or spend a day playing outside without being allowed to watch TV for a week?

93. *Would you rather*...try to ride a rhino, or swim with hungry hypos?

94. *Would you rather*...hug a lion, or kiss an alligator?

95. *Would you rather*...have a pony but be forced to clean after it, or have a pet snake and have your mom take care of it instead?

96. *Would you rather*...say that your dog ate your homework, or that a pigeon stole it from you?

97. *Would you rather*...go to the zoo every week, or get to see the wildlife of Africa once a year?

98. *Would you rather*...make a time machine that can take you to the future, or travel to the past?

99. *Would you rather*...become friends with an intelligent robot, or get a jet pack for your birthday?

100. *Would you rather*...make summer holidays longer for three months, or prolong Christmas holidays for three weeks?

101. *Would you rather*...eat only vegetables forever, or only eat fruit for good?

102. *Would you rather*...understand dogs, or be able to speak with cats?

103. *Would you rather*...walk on your hands and feet for a week, or jump on one leg for a single weekend?

104. *Would you rather*...switch roles with your teacher for a week, or switch roles with your mom and dad for the same time period?

105. *Would you rather*...invent something useful, or invent something cool?

106. *Would you rather*...go to school in your pajamas for a day, or have your mom follow you to all your classes the entire day?

107. *Would you rather*...organize a snowball fight, or a water gun battle?

108. *Would you rather*...play laser tag every day with your friends, or play your favorite game every day by yourself?

109. *Would you rather*...become friends with the Easter Bunny, or become friends with Santa Clause?

110. *Would you rather*...learn how to fly a plane, or learn how to skipper a ship?

111. *Would you rather*...have a trampoline and be allowed on it every weekend, or a treehouse and be allowed in it twice a month?

112. *Would you rather*...sail with Vikings or sail with explorers?

113. *Would you rather*...become a superhero but that no one may ever know, or be the most famous ninja?

114. *Would you rather*...eat baby food for a week or wear a diaper for two days?

115. *Would you rather*...forget how to speak, or forget how to read?

116. *Would you rather*...only watch comedy movies, or only watch superhero movies?

117. *Would you rather*...become a character from your favorite book, or a character from your favorite comic book?

118. *Would you rather*...spend an entire day with a monkey in a cage, or an hour with a snake outside a cage?

119. *Would you rather*...have the aliens visit our planet, or go visit the aliens yourself?

120. *Would you rather*...become a teacher, or go to school three years longer than supposed to?

121. *Would you rather*...have your skin covered in scales, or have a slimy frog-like skin?

122. *Would you rather*...give up burgers, or give up candy forever?

123. *Would you rather*...always make it an hour early everywhere you go, or always be 30 minutes late?

124. *Would you rather*...have three sisters, or have three brothers?

125. *Would you rather*...know everything about any object you touch or be able to predict the weather changes?

126. *Would you rather*...have free rides in every amusement park you go, or have a key that opens any door?

127. *Would you rather*...live on a boat, or live in a tree house?

128. *Would you rather*...know your
   future, or know everyone else's
   future but your own?

129. *Would you rather*...climb the
   tallest point on Earth, or dive into
   the deepest corner of the ocean?

130. *Would you rather*...jump over a
   simmering volcano, or over a pit full
   of snakes?

131. *Would you rather*...discover an
   animal that no one had ever seen, or
   discover a cure for all illnesses?

132. *Would you rather*...open a
   magical box, or open magical
   doors?

133. *Would you rather*...live in the
   present, or live 3,000 years ago?

134. *Would you rather*...never have to
   answer questions that you don't
   like, or have everyone honestly

answer any question that you ask
them?

135. *Would you rather*...sing along to
every song you hear no matter
where you are, or be forced to dance
whenever a song comes up?

136. *Would you rather*...live in a world
where there's only night time, or in
a world where the sun never sets?

137. *Would you rather*...have an
uncomfortable blanket but the most
comfortable pillow, or have an
uncomfortable pillow but the
comfiest blanket?

138. *Would you rather*...be the main
character in the last movie you saw,
or the main character from the last
book you read?

139. *Would you rather*...never leave
the place where you live, or move
every year to a new city?

140. *Would you rather*...have a beard of bees, or hair of wasps?

141. *Would you rather*...have your skin changing colors based on your mood, or say everything you think aloud?

142. *Would you rather*...never be able to tell a lie, or not be able to tell when someone is lying to you?

143. *Would you rather*...travel through time in a random year every time you start coughing, or appear at a random place any time you sneeze?

144. *Would you rather*...have all dogs dislike, or have all cats dislike you?

145. *Would you rather*...have your index fingers tied together for a day, or have to walk with your shoelaces untied for a week?

146. *Would you rather*...give up breakfast, or give up dinner?

147. *Would you rather*...know how to speak all languages in the world, or know how to play any instrument?

148. *Would you rather*...have year-long rainy days, or year-long snowing days?

149. *Would you rather*...eat only mayonnaise for breakfast every morning, or apply it on your hair every night?

150. *Would you rather*...be stranded on a desert island all alone, or be stuck on an island with someone that never stops talking?

151. *Would you rather*...have no toys rather than your favorite toy, or have many toys, but not your favorite?

152. Would you rather...live without TV, or without video games?

153. Would you rather...answer everything in riddles, or be asked questions only in form of riddles?

154. Would you rather...be allowed to wear only one color for the rest of your life, or wear the same shoes forever?

155. Would you rather...have plenty of time but nothing to do, or have plenty to do but not enough time?

156. Would you rather...be the strongest person on Earth, or the smartest?

157. Would you rather...have a robot that cleans your room or have a machine that always prepares what you like to eat?

158. *Would you rather*...be forced to wear a big pink hat everywhere you go, or wear super-sized yellow pants?

159. *Would you rather*...become a bird, or an animal of your choice?

160. *Would you rather*...read other people's minds, or be very persuasive?

161. *Would you rather*...only cheeseburgers for a week under a condition that your breakfast is kale juice, or only eat pizza if your breakfast is spinach soup?

162. *Would you rather*...read a book, or write a book?

163. *Would you rather*...explore ancient cities, or solve detective mysteries?

164. *Would you rather...*wear a
cowbell around your neck for a
weak, or spend a day working on a
farm?

165. *Would you rather...*eat an entire
cake and a single cheeseburger, or a
dozen cheeseburgers and a piece of
cake?

166. *Would you rather...*win a trip to
an exotic island, or let your friend
win a life-long supply of candy?

167. *Would you rather...* find a genie
that can grant you only one wish, or
kiss a frog that can grant you three
wishes?

168. *Would you rather...*eat a whole
apple with warms in it, or drink a
glass of spoiled milk?

169. *Would you rather...* have a cat
that acts like a dog, or a dog that
acts like a cat?

170. *Would you rather...* be able to undo bad decisions, or predict the outcome of every decision you are about to make?

171. *Would you rather...* be the fastest runner, or be able to fly but be very slow when flying?

172. *Would you rather...* have an endless supply of ice cream, or an endless supply of pizza?

173. *Would you rather...* be a giant, or a very tiny elf?

174. *Would you rather...* travel into the past and meet your great-great-grandparents, or travel to future and meet your great-great-grandchildren?

175. *Would you rather...* become a dentist, or go to the dentist every week?

176. *Would you rather...* have no eyebrows, or have no eyelashes?

177. *Would you rather...* have a long tongue, or a long nose?

178. *Would you rather...* smell like a fish, or look like a fish?

179. *Would you rather...* have double desserts after dinner, or skip school on Mondays?

180. *Would you rather...* eat a spoonful of ants, or a single grasshopper?

181. *Would you rather...* have all your clothes too big, or too small?

182. *Would you rather...* have no hair, or have no teeth?

183. Would you rather... lay still when it's raining, or be forced to sit through the days when it's snowing?

184. Would you rather... only use salt for your food, or only use sugar?

185. Would you rather... never to see the ending of your favorite show, or having to watch 30 minutes long commercials whenever you are watching your show?

186. Would you rather... never have the need to go to the bathroom, or never to feel hungry again?

187. Would you rather... spend a day walking a cockroach, or be followed by a pack of mosquitos everywhere you go for a day?

188. Would you rather... eat dog food for a week, or sleep in a dog house for a week?

189. *Would you rather...* have donut Wednesdays, or pancake Mondays?

190. *Would you rather...* lose the sense of taste, or lose the sense of smell?

191. *Would you rather...* only eat cookies, or never to eat cookies again?

192. *Would you rather...* climb a mountain on your way to school, or swim a river?

193. *Would you rather...* always say what you think, or never express your opinion again?

194. *Would you rather...* go to bed in your shoes, or only be allowed to wear sandals everywhere you go?

195. *Would you rather...* be average in everything, or be the best at only one thing?

196. *Would you rather...* know how every movie ends before you see it, or forget the ending of every movie you see?

197. *Would you rather...* sweat all the time, or sneeze every hour?

198. *Would you rather...* have no pets at all, or have too many pets?

199. *Would you rather...* swim with a whale, or take a really deep dive into the ocean?

200. *Would you rather...* feel what other people feel, or have everyone feel what you feel?

201. *Would you rather...* forget to put on a shirt before you take off to school, or forget to put on your shoes?

202. *Would you rather...* have all your shirts be too tight, or all your shoes too big?

203. *Would you rather...* switch hairstyles with one of your grandparents, or switch clothes with your grandma?

204. *Would you rather...* be stung by a wasp, or be bitten by a spider?

205. *Would you rather...* have a pet raccoon, or have a pet badger?

206. *Would you rather...* wear clothes in the shower, or wear your underpants over your clothes?

207. *Would you rather...* spend a day with someone you don't like, or not be allowed to see your friends for a week?

208. *Would you rather...* have a flying car, or see stars through your bedroom ceiling?

209. *Would you rather...* be able to see great in the dark, or hear silent sounds that no one else can?

210. *Would you rather...*be allowed to watch only your favorite movie forever, or be allowed to listen only your favorite song for good?

211. *Would you rather...* spend the night in a creepy house, or be alone in the woods for a week?

212. *Would you rather...* never to eat spaghetti again, or only eat spaghetti forever?

213. *Would you rather...* dye your hair green, or have your toenails permanently dyed red?

214. *Would you rather...* eat a mud cake, or drink dirty water?

215. *Would you rather...* get plenty of gifts that you didn't wish for, or have a single wish granted?

216. *Would you rather...* sleep without a pillow, or sleep in clothes you wore during the day?

217. *Would you rather...* sneeze whenever you hear someone sneeze, or fall asleep shortly whenever someone yawns?

218. *Would you rather...* bark at people when angry, or meow at people when you need something?

219. *Would you rather...* be able to solve the most difficult math task, or solve a riddle that no one can solve?

220. *Would you rather...* become the world's most famous magician, or have real magic powers that no one may know about?

221. *Would you rather...* eat all your meals with your fingers, or sit on the floor while eating?

222. *Would you rather...* become a lion for a day, or a wolf?

223. *Would you rather...* have no toothbrush, or have no toothpaste?

224. *Would you rather...* have eleven toes, or eleven fingers?

225. *Would you rather...* be the best at spelling, or at solving math problems?

226. *Would you rather...* have a magical ring that can take you anywhere you like, or a magic flying carpet?

227. *Would you rather...* own an amusement park, or have free rides at a water park?

228. *Would you rather...* wear stinky socks on your feet for a week, or clean socks on your hands for two days?

229. *Would you rather...* wear gloves in the summer, or wear sandals during winter?

230. *Would you rather...* be very short but fast, or very tall but slow?

231. *Would you rather...* have a glass that always fills up with your favorite drink, or a plate that always has your favorite food on it?

232. *Would you rather...* become a pop star singer, or a rock star guitarist?

233. *Would you rather...* swim for an entire day, or walk barefoot the whole day?

234. *Would you rather...* always wear unmatching socks, or wear unmatching colors?

235. *Would you rather...* look strong but be actually weak, or look weak but be actually strong?

236. *Would you rather...* launch a rocket to the Moon, or be launched in a rocket to the Moon?

237. *Would you rather...* become good friends with someone you didn't like before, or lose one of your best friends?

238. *Would you rather...* live in a zoo for a week, or live in a museum for a week?

239. *Would you rather...* stay your age forever, or grow up overnight?

240. *Would you rather...* wash your hair with ketchup, or take a shower with mustard instead of shampoo?

241. *Would you rather...* have a duck-sized horse, or a horse-sized duck?

242. *Would you rather...* have butterflies follow you everywhere, or become friends with spiders?

243. *Would you rather...* have shark teeth, or frog legs?

244. *Would you rather...* sound like a dolphin when laughing, or sound like an elephant when yawning?

245. *Would you rather...* always wear sunglasses at night, or always wear a diving suit at your birthday parties?

246. *Would you rather...* huge lips, or a really tiny nose?

247. *Would you rather...* give up your pet, or your computer?

248. *Would you rather...* be a dragon, or have a pet dragon?

249. *Would you rather...* get stuck in a public bathroom for an hour, or stuck in an elevator for two hours?

250. *Would you rather...*become a firefighter of a police officer?

251. *Would you rather...* become a ballerina, or become an actress?

252. *Would you rather...* only be able to talk silently so barely anyone can hear you, or only be able to talk really loudly?

253. *Would you rather...* have yellow teeth, or have half your teeth missing?

254. *Would you rather...* have an entire month without your computer, or a month without your best friends?

255. *Would you rather...* smell like a skunk, or have skunk fur instead of hair?

256. *Would you rather...* take a slide down a rainbow, or take a ride on a cloud?

257. *Would you rather...* hear the drums when you trip and fall, or hear an alarm when you do something wrong?

258. *Would you rather...* only eat and drink cold food and beverage during winter, or drink and eat hot food and beverage in the summer?

259. *Would you rather...* smile at the end of everything you say, or wink before anything you say no matter what it is?

260. *Would you rather...* say "Never!" aloud when your teacher says what's for homework, or say the same thing to your mom when she says it's time to go to bed?

261. *Would you rather...* wear little bells around your ankles at all times, or have really long nails that you can't clip?

262. *Would you rather...* help someone solve a problem, or babysit a one-year-old for an entire day?

263. *Would you rather...* never have a chewing gum again, or only chew tasteless gum?

264. *Would you rather...* live in a
world where computers were never
invented, or in a world where toilet
paper was never invented?

265. *Would you rather...* become a
treasure hunter, or a pirate?

266. *Would you rather...* go snow
skiing, or water skiing?

267. *Would you rather...* spend a day
with pandas, or spend a day with
koala bears?

268. *Would you rather...* race a deer,
or race a horse?

269. *Would you rather...* enter a
jumping competition against a frog,
or against a kangaroo?

270. *Would you rather...* have a pet
parrot, or a pet lizard?

271. *Would you rather...* hug a porcupine, or hug a wild bear?

272. *Would you rather...* live in a big and crowded city, or live on a countryside?

273. *Would you rather...* have lunch with your favorite movie star, or your favorite movie character?

274. *Would you rather...* get your face stained so you can't clean it for a day, or have a stained shirt for hours before you are able to change clothes?

275. *Would you rather...* wear shoes on opposite feet, or wear someone else's used socks?

276. *Would you rather...* clean crocodile's teeth, or give a bath to a snake?

277. *Would you rather...* camp in the mountains, or in your own backyard?

278. *Would you rather...* brush your teeth with soap, or wash your hands with toothpaste?

279. *Would you rather...* watch a black and white movie, or watch a TV program for babies for three hours?

280. *Would you rather...* eat a plate full of boiled broccoli, or a plate of cabbage soup?

281. *Would you rather...* lose memory of who you are, or lose memory of who your best friends are?

282. *Would you rather...* have pillow fights, or water balloon fights?

283. *Would you rather...* smell stinky shoes, or rotten eggs?

284. *Would you rather...* go to the cinema every week, or have sleepovers with your friends twice a month?

285. *Would you rather...* be sleepy for a week, or feel hungry for a week?

286. *Would you rather...* create a new cool toy that everyone will love, or make a great movie that everyone would want to watch?

287. *Would you rather...* go to any place in the world of your choice, or buy the toy that you've always wanted?

288. *Would you rather...* go to the dentist or to the doctor?

289. *Would you rather...* go to school on the back of a dinosaur, or on the back of a unicorn?

290. *Would you rather...* make a fort out of snow, or build a fort out of pillows?

291. *Would you rather...* skip one year of school, or go to school only three days a week?

292. *Would you rather...* have bananas instead of fingers, or a carrot instead of nose?

293. *Would you rather...* eat a pound of tomatoes, or a pound of cherries?

294. *Would you rather...* eat a raw potato, or a whole lemon?

295. *Would you rather...* have three months of summer holidays, or go to school during summer and have the rest of the year turn into holidays?

296. *Would you rather...* all your food tasted like pizza, or all your food tasted like ice cream?

297. *Would you rather...* have an alligator pond in your backyard, or have a family of bears in your backyard?

298. *Would you rather...* be a cartoon character of your choice, or become a movie star that you like?

299. *Would you rather...* take a bus or a car ride, or take a walk?

300. *Would you rather...* only have black clothes, or only have white clothes?

301. *Would you rather...* meet a fairy, or meet a genie?

302. *Would you rather...* join a debate club, or join chess club?

303. *Would you rather*... be the
   youngest among your siblings, or

304. *Would you rather*... listen to
   someone reading a book, or read a
   book by yourself?

305. *Would you rather*... climb a tall
   tree, or climb a hill?

306. *Would you rather*... never know
   where your pajamas are, or never be
   able to find your hair comb when
   you need it?

307. *Would you rather*... be able to
   find everything you have ever lost,
   or stumble upon things that other
   people lost?

308. *Would you rather*... go to a
   summer camp, or go on a vacation
   with your family?

309. *Would you rather*...make a snowman that comes to life, or make the greatest snow fort?

310. *Would you rather*... move to a new house, or go to a new school?

311. *Would you rather*... become a superhero sidekick, or become a superhero without a sidekick?

312. *Would you rather*... would you rather have three superpowers, or have numerous cool gadgets?

313. *Would you rather*...crawl for an entire day, or crouch instead of walking for a day?

314. *Would you rather*... travel in a car, or fly by a plane?

315. *Would you rather*... skip Christmas, or skip Halloween?

316. *Would you rather...* play board games with your friends, or play a video game by yourself?

317. *Would you rather...* lose your piggy bank, or lose your one-week allowance?

318. *Would you rather...* iron all your clothes, or fold all your clothes?

319. *Would you rather...* live in a house with no faucet water, or in a house with no electricity?

320. *Would you rather...* pick all your clothes by yourself, or let your mom pick instead of you?

321. *Would you rather...* have a tomato smoothie, or potato milkshake?

322. *Would you rather...* eat home-cooked dinner, or have takeout dinners from restaurants?

323. *Would you rather*... speak an imaginary language that only you and your friends understand, or learn three new languages?

324. *Would you rather*... have a nanny that is too strict on bedtime, or a nanny that is terrible at cooking?

325. *Would you rather*...have breakfast in bed on Saturdays, or get to choose Saturday dinners?

326. *Would you rather*... have a runny nose, or a sore throat?

327. *Would you rather*... stay at home for weekends, or go on weekend trips with your family?

328. *Would you rather*... have a pinball machine in your bedroom, or have mini-golf field in your backyard?

329. *Would you rather...* have lunch with the President, or have lunch with the Queen?

330. *Would you rather...* talk nonsense for a day, or walk backward for a day?

331. *Would you rather...* wash your hands 20 times a day, or wash your feet 5 times a day?

332. *Would you rather...* never get any presents, or only get presents that you don't like or need?

333. *Would you rather...* eat a tiny chili pepper, or eat a spoonful of ground pepper?

334. *Would you rather...* be tickled, or feel itchy?

335. *Would you rather...* meet a spaghetti monster, or eat three plates of spaghetti for dinner?

336. *Would you rather...* never have anyone share anything with you, or share everything?

337. *Would you rather...*have squirrel's tale, or rabbit teeth?

338. *Would you rather...* understand what babies are saying, or understand what cats are meowing?

339. *Would you rather...* publish a video of yourself goofing around, or dance like a chicken in front of your friends?

340. *Would you rather...* be followed by a goose everywhere you go for a day, or run from an angry goat for an hour?

341. *Would you rather...* have transparent skin, or have green skin like an alien?

342. *Would you rather...* wear clown's wig for a day, or have your hair turned into cotton candy for an entire day?

343. *Would you rather...* transform into an ant, or into an anteater?

344. *Would you rather...* drink a glass of apple vinegar, or eat two spoons of minced garlic?

345. *Would you rather...* live in a world full of robots, or in a world full of aliens?

346. *Would you rather...* have a friend tell one of your secrets, or be forced to tell a secret your best friend told you?

347. *Would you rather...* have your mom talk to you in baby voice in front of the whole school, or have a friend embarrass you at school?

348. Would you rather... play hide and seeks, or play dodgeball?

349. Would you rather... go camping, or go ship cruising?

350. Would you rather... sing in a moving elevator full of strangers, or dance while walking down the stairs in a shopping mall?

351. Would you rather... wake up as the fastest flying animal, or wake up as the fastest running animal?

352. Would you rather... live in a cave with a family of fruit bats, or live in a cave alone?

353. Would you rather... have food spilled on your shoes, or a soda spilled on your clothes?

354. Would you rather... try to hide whenever you are watching a scary movie, or tremble whenever a scary movie is on?

355. *Would you rather...* listen only to your grandparents' music, or only listen to a single song of your choice?

356. *Would you rather...* be forced to start whistling whenever a song comes up, or snap your fingers to every song you hear?

357. *Would you rather...* wear itchy clothes, or wear itchy shoes?

358. *Would you rather...* have a curse of horrible haircuts, or a curse of horrible outfits?

359. *Would you rather...* have a blanket that reads goodnight stories, or a pillow that plays sounds of the ocean?

360. *Would you rather...* drink warm milk before bedtime, or cold cocoa after you wake up?

361. *Would you rather...* meet a tooth fairy, or get more candy for Halloween?

362. *Would you rather...* have a pie splashed into your face, or have a bucket of mud splashed all over your clothes?

363. *Would you rather...* share a room with a sleep talker, or with a sleepwalker?

364. *Would you rather...* be 2 years older than you are, or 2 years younger than you are now?

365. *Would you rather...* get over your worst fear or have one dream come true?

366. *Would you rather...* have more time allowed for playing video games, or have longer weekends?

367. *Would you rather...* get your head stuck in a circus' lion jaws, or be launched out of a cannon in a circus?

368. *Would you rather...* read 50 book pages in a day, or watch TV for 5 hours straight?

369. *Would you rather...* ride an elephant-sized snail, or keep a snail sized elephant as a pet?

370. *Would you rather...* live on your own island with only people you like, or become a president of your country?

371. *Would you rather...* have no ways of warming up when it's cold, or have no way of cooling down when it's hot?

372. *Would you rather...* never to be able to tell a lie again, or never to be able to tell the truth again?

373. *Would you rather...* tell on a friend who did something wrong, or take blame for something you didn't do?

374. *Would you rather...*be forced to laugh at anyone wearing a yellow shirt, or be forced to start dancing instead of saying "Hi!"?

375. *Would you rather...* to be able to move objects with your mind, or to create fire with your bare hands?

376. *Would you rather...* have a cloggy nose for a week, or a runny nose?

377. *Would you rather...* become a tennis player, or become a baseball player?

378. Would you rather... needy baby sister, or an overly protective older brother?

379. Would you rather... half-human half-bat, or half-human half-spider?

380. Would you rather... have a smart house that cleans itself and talks to you, or an elf that always helps around?

381. Would you rather... make friends with a group of squirrels, or with a group of raccoons?

382. Would you rather... live with a stinky troll, or with a really loud ogre?

383. Would you rather... be raised by gorillas, or raised by tigers?

384. Would you rather... eat pizza crust without the toppings, or pizza toppings without the crust?

385. *Would you rather...* develop an allergy to chocolate, or be allergic to dogs?

386. *Would you rather...* hold your breath for a minute, or run without stopping for two minutes?

387. *Would you rather...* spend a day at a library, or a day at an art gallery?

388. *Would you rather...* become friends with someone noisy, or be friends with someone who is nosy?

389. *Would you rather...* meet a time traveler, or a space traveler?

390. *Would you rather...* live on Mars, or live on Saturn?

391. *Would you rather...* be a kid, or an adult?

392. *Would you rather...* carry an umbrella only on sunny days, or have an umbrella with you at all times?

393. *Would you rather...* sleep during the day as bats do, or sleep during winters like bears?

394. *Would you rather...* grow your own food, or make your own shoes?

395. *Would you rather...* have an impossible case of hiccups for an entire day, or not be able to blink for a whole day?

396. *Would you rather...* have tickling mustache on your face, or a joke-telling beard on your chin?

397. *Would you rather...* have an identical twin, or have an inseparable friend?

398. *Would you rather...* be spooky for a day, or get spooked for two days?

399. *Would you rather...* share your room with slugs, or share your house with snails?

400. *Would you rather...* take a path to another world through a rabbit hole, or enter a magical world through a closet?

401. *Would you rather...* ask "Would you rather...", or be asked "Would you rather..."?